THE WHALE

a play

TODD ALCOTT

THE WHALE

a play

by Todd Alcott

from *Moby-Dick* by Herman Melville

INTRODUCTION

Herman Melville's *Moby-Dick* has been adapted hundreds of times. The last thing the world needs is another adaptation of *Moby-Dick*.

Here is another adaptation of *Moby-Dick*.

I decided to write an adaptation of *Moby-Dick* because all the other adaptations are, frankly, terrible. Not one of them – not one – captures the novel's weirdness, its terror, its sense of dread and dark poetry.

To say nothing of its humor. Melville is a screamingly funny writer, much funnier than Shakespeare or Dickens, and there are moments in *Moby-Dick* that are clearly meant to shoot right past "adventure story" and "great American novel" to land at some strange netherland of surreal comedy.

What I find most strange about every adaptation of *Moby-Dick* is that not one even captures its basic plot. *Moby-Dick* is about a man who hires a group of sailors to perform a job, and then, once he has them helpless and at his will, turns the workplace - which happens to be a ship - into a literal death cult. Ahab makes it plain that they are all headed to their deaths for the sake of his personal vengeance, and he succeeds in getting them all to go along with him. Cheerfully. Enthusiastically.

In a strange way, any one of Disney's *Pirates of the Caribbean* movies, with their magically evil captains and their crews of cursed, comical sailors, comes closer to capturing the spirit of *Moby-Dick*. So many times while watching those movies I've wished they had simply cut out Johnny Depp and the starcrossed lovers just concentrated on the dynamics of one of the colorful cursed crews.

I had to adapt *Moby-Dick* because it's about my father. My father married my mother and they had four children. She put up with his narcissism and abuse under the expectation that he would remain employed at an advertising agency and that he would support the family in upper-middle-class style to the end of our days. Then, one day, he quit his job at the advertising agency and, just like Ahab, changed the rules of the game when it was too late for anyone to get off the boat. He started his own business, squandered every dime my family had saved, plunged us deep into debt, forced my mother into working two jobs to support us, and finally drove her to her death. As a grade-A blue-ribbon narcissist, he demanded constant praise and support for anything he did, no matter how wrong-headed or damaging it was. In the end, all his children abandoned him and he came home one day to find all of the family belongings in the front yard and the door locked by the sheriff.

There is a scene near the end of *Moby-Dick* where Ahab, for a moment, sees the error of his ways and almost turns the ship around. But he can't, because he's come all this way, this is who he is. He knows he's going to die, he knows it's going to kill all his men and destroy his ship, but he has to do it. I freely weep every time I read that scene, or even contemplate it, because it describes my father so precisely, and I live in the fear that it also describes myself. So many men sacrifice themselves and their families for the sake of an unknowable, unreachable goal.

And that, in the end, is what *Moby-Dick* is about. These days we call it "toxic masculinity" but it's really just common vanity that makes men elevate their personal obsessions into wrestling matches with angels and demons. I end my play at the Pequod's rail and Ahab's revelation because, for me, everything that happens in the novel afterward is decorative.

This play is unique in my work as it presents considerable challenges in staging. I don't pretend to have answers for how to get the deck of the Pequod onto a stage, much less how to stage a whaling battle or a pitching sea. Puppets? Bolts of cloth? A slideshow? I have no idea. The important thing is the emotional core, the peculiar, heart-stopping strangeness of the mystery of *Moby-Dick* and the hunt for the white whale.

ONE

(Ahab's cabin, night. There is a scream, off. Starbuck, Stubb and Flask carry in a thrashing Ahab, who has just been fished out of the ocean. He lacks a leg. They put him into his bed.)

AHAB. Aaaagh! Aaaagh!

STARBUCK. It's all right, Captain. You're all right.

AHAB. Is he dead? Did I kill him?

STARBUCK. He got away, captain.

AHAB. Got away? Got *away*?

STUBB. He's a big fish, sir, he –

AHAB. We have to go *after* him! Set sails!

FLASK. We're not going anywhere tonight, sir –

STARBUCK. Just lie down, captain.

AHAB. He, he smashed by boat! Is my harpooneer –

STUBB. He's fine.

STARBUCK. Just lie down, sir –

AHAB. Did you *see* him? Did you – tell me you *saw* him!

FLASK. We saw him.

STARBUCK. We'll go after him tomorrow.

AHAB. He, he, he thought he had me. But he didn't. He thought he did but he didn't.

STARBUCK. No sir.

AHAB. Bastard thought he had me. But not Ahab. He didn't have Ahab. No.

STUBB. No sir.

AHAB. There isn't a whale alive who can get Ahab. No one – AAGHH! WHERE'S MY LEG?! WHAT HAPPENED TO MY LEG?! MR. STARBUCK? WHAT HAPPENED TO MY LEG?!! AAAAGH!

(Blackout.)

TWO

(Ishmael addresses the audience.)

ISHMAEL. So I thought I'd go to sea.

There's nothing "weird" about that, nothing "strange", nothing "peculiar" about that. People go to sea. Men are drawn to the sea. The sea, water –

New York City, lunch hour. What happens? Battery Park, people go and stand by the water. Look at a map: where do they put the cities? By the water. Guy paints a picture, nice bucolic landscape, what's in the middle of the picture? A lake. A stream. A pond. Why not?

So I thought I'd go to sea. Big deal. It was either that or kill myself. Or kill somebody else.

But that's not the thing. The thing, the thing is, I am crazy about whales. I am nuts, I am gaga, I am absolutely round the bend about whales. Can't get enough of them whales. Stories, pictures, books, scrimshaw, if it's whales I like it.

So perfect: I go to Nantucket to get myself booked on a

whaling boat. Me and my new best friend Queequeg – he's from the South Pacific (it's a long story) – we decide on this ship the Pequod.

(Lights up on the Pequod. The deck bustles with activity.)

It's an amazing ship. Not the biggest, not the nicest, not the fastest, but definitely the coolest. Everything on the ship is made of whale-bone! The pins are teeth, hammered into boards of bone. The tiller is a jawbone. It's a death ship. The thing is a death ship, a cannibal ship, it's a monster, it's a flesh-eating zombie ship. It's a death-ship, and that's the kind of ship I want to be on.

THREE

(A cabin on the Pequod. Peleg at a desk. Bildad reads the bible.)

ISHMAEL. Are you the captain?

PELEG. What if I was?

ISMAEL. I want to join on.

PELEG. You're not from Nantucket.

ISMAEL. No.

PELEG. You know whaling?

ISMAEL. No sir. But I'm a quick study. I was in the merchant marines...

PELEG. Merchant marines my ass. Talk to me about the merchant marines, I'll rip off your leg, I promise. What are you, a pirate? A wanted man? You robbed your last captain? You get to sea, you murder your officers?

ISHMAEL. No sir. No.

PELEG. Then why whaling?

ISHMAEL. I – I don't – I like – I want to see whales. I want to see whaling.

PELEG. You want to see whaling. Have you seen Ahab?

ISHMAEL. Who?

PELEG. Ahab.

ISMAEL. Who is that?

PELEG. Christ. – Ahab is the captain of the Pequod.

ISHMAEL. I – I'm sorry. I thought you were.

PELEG. Christ no. I'm Peleg – this is Bildad. We own the ship. And before you get all hopped up about "whaling", I suggest you take a look at Ahab.

ISHMAEL. W-why is that, sir?

PELEG. You'll know when you look at him.

ISHMAEL. I-I see sir.

PELEG. He's got one leg, how's that?

ISHMAEL. Oh. Really. What happened to the, the – what happened to him?

PELEG. Why don't you take a guess.

ISHMAEL. Um…a whale? Um, took it?

(Pause.)

PELEG. Ate it. A whale ate it.

ISHMAEL. Yes. Well. Accidents happen, sir.

PELEG. It wasn't an accident.

ISHMAEL. Excuse me?

PELEG. It wasn't an accident.

ISHMAEL. Uh, right.

PELEG. You've never been to sea –

ISHMAEL. Yes sir I have. Four trips in the merch –

PELEG. Fuck the merchant marines! You want to go *whaling*?

ISHMAEL. Yes sir!

PELEG. You're ready to pitch a harpoon down a whale's throat and jump in after?

ISHMAEL. If it comes to that, yes. Although I'd rather not waste the harpoon.

PELEG. Good answer. Bildad! (Bildad grunts.) You readin' that damn book again? You been readin' scripture for thirty years now, how far ya got? (Bildad looks up from the book.) Guy here says he's our man.

BILDAD. Yes?

PELEG. Says he's the one we want. What do you think?

(Pause.)

BILDAD. He'll do.

(He goes back to reading, murmuring with the text.)

PELEG. Well then that's that. Sign here. Now: your wage. Bildad? (Bildad grunts.) His lay.

BILDAD. (not looking up) One seven hundred seventy-seventh. "Where moth and rust do corrupt, but *lay...*"

PELEG. For Christ's sake, Bildad! You want to *swindle* him?

BILDAD. One seven hundred seventy-seventh. "For where your treasure is, there will your heart be also..."

PELEG. (sighs) He's ridiculous. I'll put you down for three hundred. (to Bildad) Three hundred.

(Bildad looks up. Pause.)

BILDAD. Well aren't you a kindly old fool. And whose money *is* that you're so generously giving away? Yours? Mine? No. It belongs to the widows and orphans who have shares in this ship. Your act of benevolence toward this boy you've never seen before in your life takes bread out of their mouths.

PELEG. God damn it Bildad! If I did everything you told me to, I'd have a conscience heavy enough to sink a ship!

BILDAD. Mr. Peleg, the weight of your conscience is not my concern. I suspect, however, from your lack of penitence, that it is heavy enough to drag you down to the fiery pit.

PELEG. Fiery pit! Fiery pit! So I'm going to Hell. Is that it? Go on, say it again. Say it again, I'll swallow a live goat with his hair and horns on! God damn you! God *damn* you! (Pause. To Ishmael --) Well. That's over. I'll put you down for three hundred.

ISHMAEL. Thank you sir. Could I – do you think maybe I could see Captain Ahab?

PELEG. Why? You've already signed on –

ISHMAEL. I know. I just want to – you mentioned –

PELEG. You want to see Ahab?

ISHMAEL. Yes.

PELEG. Well you can't.

ISHMAEL. Oh.

PELEG. He's sick.

ISHMAEL. What's the matter with him?

PELEG. I don't know. He won't come out.

ISHMAEL. If he's sick –

PELEG. He's not *sick* –

ISHMAEL. No?

PELEG. No. But he's not well. He won't see me, he certainly won't see you. He's a – he's a strange man. Don't get me wrong, he's a great guy. A great, God-fearing, Godless, Godly son-of-a-bitch. Doesn't talk much. But when he talks, you listen. He's done it all, knows colleges and cannibals. He knows things deeper than the ocean. And his lance is the sharpest on the island. He's not a Peleg and he's not a Bildad. He's Ahab. Another Ahab was king, you know.

ISHMAEL. Uh, yes. A, a very bad king, if I remember correctly.

PELEG. Yes. Well.

ISHMAEL. I mean, a *really* bad king.

PELEG. Come here, boy. Here. Listen: Ahab did not name himself. His mother named him. And she was crazy, died a year after he was born. And maybe that means something and maybe it doesn't. But I'm telling you Ahab is a good man. Okay: last trip, he went a little crazy; so what? He'd lost his leg, you know? So he's a little moody. A lot moody. All right, he's a savage. But I'd rather sail with a moody captain than a laughing one. Besides, he has a wife! Beautiful, and a son, a little boy. So how bad could he be?

(Blackout.)

FOUR

(Ishmael addresses the audience.)

ISHMAEL. And we're off. Christmas day, for those keen on symbolism.

Now here's something interesting about the Pequod. Ahab, the captain, is white. Starbuck and Stubb and Flask, the mates, are white. But the harpooneers? The ones who actually kill the whales? Not white. Listen:

(Queequeg addresses the audience.)

QUEEQUEG. My name is Queequeg. I come from an island in the South Pacific. I was a prince of my people, the first son of the King. I would have been King. But when I saw my first whaler? That was it for me. I climbed on board and never looked back.

(Tashtego addresses the audience.)

TASHTEGO. My name is Tashtego. I'm an Indian from Martha's Vineyard, the Western part, Gay Head, one of the last villages left. There's a lot of us in Nantucket now, in whaling. The white people call us "Gayheaders". Men in my village used to hunt moose, but we can't do that any more. Now we climb aboard ships and hunt whales.

(Dagoo addresses the audience.)

DAGOO. My name is Dagoo. I've never been anywhere except Africa, Nantucket, and wherever my ship puts into harbor. I'm six-foot-five. My earrings are solid gold. I don't wear shoes. Never could. For some reason, white people are scared of me.

ISHMAEL. We have a number of Negroes. Pip is from Alabama, but we have a number of Islanders: Jamaicans, Haitians, Bahamians, what have you. For some reason the islanders are good whalers, I don't know why. What else do we have? On a purely informal investigation, I found a Dutchman, a Frenchman, a Icelander, a Maltese, a Sicilian, a Long Islander, an Azorean, a Chinese, a Manxman, a Lascarian, a Tahitian, a Portuguese, a Dane, an Englishman, a Spaniard, and one guy from Belfast.

Now I want to clear something up. People have this "idea" about whaling, that we're "butchers", that we're somehow "below" decent society. Yes, we're butchers. We kill noble beasts. But so do armies. So do generals. When a general wipes out a thousand men, he's a hero. But when a harpooneer brings down a whale, brings you oil and spermaceti, brings you jobs and income and trade by putting his life on the line by facing the most terrifying creature on the planet, he's a "butcher". Your candles, your lanterns, every light burning on this planet, your perfume, your skin cream, the bones in your pretty corsets, seven million dollars in trade in 1851 in America *alone*. *That's* what whaling is.

But of course what you want to see is Ahab. "Where's Ahab?

The mysterious Ahab? We don't care about you, we don't care about the demographics of the crew, the economics of whaling. We want to see crazy old Ahab!"

You're not alone. I have the same problem. Where's Ahab? He's not around. Days, weeks go by, no Ahab. I'm thinking we don't *have* a captain.

But then one morning, there he is. Standing on the quarter-deck, looking out to sea.

(And there he is, standing on the quarter-deck, looking out to sea.)

Silent. He talks to no one, no one talks to him. He's not sick, he doesn't look sick, but he doesn't look well either. He doesn't look…all…there, really. If you pull a man off the stake? He's still alive but his spirit is gone? That's Ahab.

He's bronze. He's made of bronze. There's a white mark that starts in his hair and goes all the way down his face. Some say it's a scar, some say it's a birthmark, some say it goes all the way down to his toes.

And then of course there's his leg. His leg. Which, of course, is not there. Missing; replaced. Made of whale-bone. So it's no surprise that he's not all there; he really isn't all there.

And that's the way it is: days, weeks, months. We take care of the ship, Ahab watches the sea. The men eat and dance and work and swear and shit and sing and piss and prepare to kill whales, and Ahab watches the sea.

And then, finally, April comes, and then May, and Ahab starts to move. A little. Not much. Not his body. But his face. His face moves. A little. In May, his face does something – on another man it might be called a smile.

And then, what do you know. He paces.

(Ahab paces.)

Up and down. All day, all night. Rarely sleeps. Up and down. Weeks. Paces. Up and down. Up and down.

(Night falls. Ahab paces. Stubb approaches.)

STUBB. Captain Ahab sir?

AHAB. Mr. Stubb?

STUBB. You think maybe you could muffle the leg, sir? We're trying to sleep.

AHAB. Oh yes. The leg. Yes. You need to sleep, yes. I forgot. Your nightly grave, yes. Fine. Back to your kennel.

STUBB. My kennel sir?

AHAB. Go away, Mr. Stubb.

STUBB. Are you calling me a dog, sir?

AHAB. No Mr. Stubb, I'm calling you a jackass. Go away.

STUBB. Captain –

AHAB. Down below or over the side, Mr. Stubb.

STUBB. Now wait just a –

AHAB. GET OUT OF HERE!!

(Blackout.)

FIVE

(Stubb with Flask.)

STUBB. He called me a dog. And a jackass. I want to hit him. I want to pray for him. I want to pray for him but I've never prayed before. Very strange. He's *very* strange. He's the strangest man I've ever met. He's crazy, that's it. He's crazy, he's mad. Doesn't sleep. And when he sleeps he doesn't sleep. He's fevered is what. He's a, he's a, he's a, I don't know what he is.

FLASK. Hm.

STUBB. I dreamed he kicked me.

FLASK. Yeah?

STUBB. But not with his foot.

FLASK. No?

STUBB. No, with his *other* foot.

FLASK. What? Oh.

STUBB. You know.

FLASK. Right.

STUBB. And I thought "What's worse? A man kicks you with his real leg or his fake leg?"

FLASK. I'm sure I don't know the answer to that.

STUBB. And I thought "Well it's only a fake leg. See? It's not a *real* leg."

FLASK. Uh huh.

STUBB. So it's not so bad.

FLASK. Right.

STUBB. So I kick him back. I kick him in the leg. The fake leg.

FLASK. Uh huh –

STUBB. And I – did I mention that he's like twenty feet tall?

FLASK. No.

STUBB. He is. And I'm kicking his fake leg, and he's like "Stop that!" Right? And I'm like "But you kicked *me*," right, and he says "You should be honored to be kicked by such a great man." See?

FLASK. Huh. And did you tell him about this dream?

STUBB. Are you out of your fucking mind?

SIX

(The deck. Men mill about. Ahab calls to Starbuck.)

AHAB. Starbuck! Everyone aft!

STARBUCK. Yes sir! (calling) All men assemble on the
aft deck!

(Ad lib as necessary.)

AHAB. You! Mast-heads! You too! (The men assemble while
Ahab paces. Finally, he stops.) What do you do when you see
a whale?

TASHTEGO. Sing out!

AHAB. Good! Then what?

DAGOO. Lower the boats!

AHAB. Good! And then?

QUEEQUEG. Chase after him!

AHAB. And then?

ALL. KILL HIM!

AHAB. Or?

ALL. OR HE KILLS US!

AHAB. Right. That is right. A dead whale or a stove boat. Good. Mr. Starbuck, get me a hammer. Men, the time has come to reveal to you your very special purpose.

You're all whalers. And I know that. You're the best, the finest, probably, in the world. And you signed onto the Pequod because you knew *she* was the finest in the world. And I know that.

But the time has come to tell you what you're really doing here. What I'm doing, what the Pequod is doing here.

Because this is not your average whale trip. We are not hunting your average whales. No. Men, you have come to hunt only one. Only one whale. A unique whale. A one-of-a-kind whale. The largest, the meanest, the most dangerous creature in the sea.

(He produces a large gold coin.)

This is a Spanish gold ounce. See? This is worth sixteen dollars. Do you see it?

Now listen: there is a whale. A white whale. With a wrinkled brow and a crooked jaw. With three holes in his starboard fluke. Whoever sees that white whale first gets this ounce of gold.

(He nails the coin to the mast.)

TASHTEGO. Are, are you talking about Moby-Dick?

AHAB. Have you seen him?

TASHTEGO. He has an unusual fan tail.

AHAB. Yes!

DAGOO. And is spout is bushy, like a plume.

AHAB. Yes!

QUEEQUEG. And he's all stuck up with irons.

AHAB. Yes!

QUEEQUEG. Twisted up like a corkscrew.

AHAB. Yes! You've seen him! You've seen him!

STARBUCK. Captain? Forgive me – isn't Moby-Dick the fish that took your leg?

AHAB. (to Starbuck) Yes. Yes it is. (To all) Yes it is. Moby-Dick took my leg. Yes. Yes, and gave me this stump, yes. Moby-Dick made me a cripple, a monster, a freak. Yes he did. And yes, I am hunting him. Around Good Hope, around the Horn, around the Norway Maelstrom, and around the flames of *Hell* if that's what it takes to kill him. And that, men, is what you're doing here. To do one thing and one thing only. Kill the white whale! Can you do it?

ALL. YES!!

AHAB. We will not stop until he spouts black blood and rolls fin out! Are you with me?!

ALL. Huzzah! Huzzah! Kill Moby-Dick! Kill Moby-Dick!

AHAB. Grog for everyone!

ALL. Huzzah!!

(Grog is poured. The men all drink.)

STARBUCK. Captain?

AHAB. Mr. Starbuck?

STARBUCK. Captain, you know that I'm not afraid of a whale.

AHAB. God yes of course!

STARBUCK. I kill whales. That's what I do. I'm a whale killer.

AHAB. Glad to hear it.

STARBUCK. It's my business. You could say. I am in the *business* of killing whales.

AHAB. I smell a "point" brewing somewhere, Mr. Starbuck.

STARBUCK. My business – this ship's business – is killing whales, sir. Not the captain's revenge. Sir. You understand, sir.

AHAB. Well Mr. Starbuck, you call me "captain", so I presume you have a basic understanding of maritime tradition, yes? That the "captain" is the guy in charge on a boat?

STARBUCK. Pardon. Sir. But the white whale – we have orders from Mr. Peleg, Mr. –

AHAB. Phuh! Those idiots –

STARBUCK. From the widows and children with *shares* in this ship – one whale is worthless –

AHAB. To them, yes. To me it's everything.

STARBUCK. Pardon sir. Again. But you don't vow revenge on a fish. The whale – he didn't know it was *your leg*, sir. You don't vow revenge on a table because you bark your shin on it.

AHAB. Appears to be.

STARBUCK. Excuse me?

AHAB. Appears to be a fish. To you and me. Less so to me. Appears to be. My job, Mr. Starbuck? "My business"? To take away that mask. To cut through that veil. We know what the whale *appears* to be. *I* am going to find out what he *is*.

STARBUCK. It's blasphemy, sir.

AHAB. To want revenge on a fish? Starbuck, I would have revenge on the *sun* if it insulted me. What are you staring at? I've got lettuce in my teeth? Wait, don't go. All right. I've made you angry. Don't take everything so personally.

Look at the crew, Mr. Starbuck. Look at them. *They* want to hunt the whale, that's what they *came* for. Look at them. Savages. Cannibals. Catholics. Blunt, stupid, glorious animals, who live and eat and die and never give anything a second thought. They love me now. Look at them laughing. They're ready to do this. They're ready to follow me to the end of the world.

STARBUCK. They are *bored*, sir. They are looking for something to *do*.

AHAB. But that's *fine*, Starbuck, who isn't? Who doesn't want to be special? Who doesn't want to feel that they're involved in a grand enterprise, a grand scheme, who doesn't want to be on the team that dares the impossible? Look at you, you wish to "know God's will". And you call *me* a blasphemer? All I want to do is kill a *whale*. Look at the crew, at what I've done to them, the fire I've lit. Now tell them you defy me.

STARBUCK. Sir –

AHAB. Go on. Tell them. Tell them what a bad idea this is. How wasteful, how impertinent, how wrong. Tell them they're going to Hell. Tell them they're going against God. Mr. Starbuck, I *am* their God. The heathens; I *am* their God.

STARBUCK. Then God help us.

(He exits.)

AHAB. Harpooneers! Bring me your weapons! Cross them! All of you! Now let me touch them. These are the blades which will kill Moby-Dick!

ALL. DEATH TO MOBY-DICK!

AHAB. Drink! Drink men! To the death of Moby-Dick!

ALL. DEATH TO MOBY-DICK!

AHAB. God hunt us if we don't hunt Moby-Dick!

ALL. DEATH TO MOBY-DICK! DEATH! DEATH! DEATH! DEATH! DEATH!

SEVEN

(Sunset. Ahab at the rail.)

AHAB. Water, water everywhere. No land. No land out here.
No land, no towns, no government, no law, no God.
Just water.

The sun comes up out of the water and then dives back in. At
noon, it sits on my head. My crown. My shining crown,
driving spikes into my brain.

I used to like the sun. Not any more. The sun mocks me
now. The sun offends me. It lights up the world, this
paradise, shows me everything I can no longer enjoy, shoves
my face in it, grinds my face against the world.

I thought it would be harder. The men. But they went off
like a string of firecrackers. Of course, to light a fire you have
to waste a match. That would be me. But I have the thought,
I have the will, and my will be done.

Starbuck thinks I'm crazy. The poor sap – he has no idea. I

am madness maddened. I am nutty, I am loco, pazzo, krank, meshuganeh. I am stupidcrazy out-of-my-skull.

But I am also a prophet. And I prophesize this: who tears me, I tear. So I am both the prophet and the fulfiller, which is more than the Gods ever were.

Cricket-players! Blind boxers! If I was a schoolboy, I'd scream at the sky "Pick on someone your own size!" But I don't say that. You knock me down, I get back up, and now you run and hide.

This is who I am. This is what I will do. It's fixed now. I couldn't change it if I tried.

EIGHT

(Men drink and clap their hands. Pip dances with his tambourine. Ad lib.)

1. Dance Pip! Dance!

2. Faster!

3. Look at him go!

4. Bang your tambourine, Pip!

5. Ring it, Pip! Dance dance dance!

(The men continue, in dumbshow. Lights up on Ishmael, who addresses the audience.)

ISHMAEL. Yes, I was there. I was standing right there with all the others. I shouted. I drank. I vowed to kill the white whale. I knew it was stupid, I knew it was crazy, I knew it was wrong, and I did it anyway. Ahab's revenge became my revenge.

And Moby-Dick became a monster. Turns out everyone on board had a Moby-Dick story, first-hand, second-hand, third-hand. He was famous. There was no end of stories about Moby-Dick. And, in the manner of fish stories, some were true and some, I'd say, were not.

One story was that Moby-Dick could be everywhere at once. That he could dive down off the coast of Greenland and be seen off the coast of Australia a day later. And maybe that's true, maybe there are secret passages under the sea we know nothing about.

One story said that Moby-Dick is immortal, that he's always been here, old as time, and cannot be killed.

He's huge, they said. The biggest ever, they said. Stuck with a dozen harpoons, still in him, they said.

They said he attacks whaling boats. He knows what they are, they are his enemy, and attacks them. People have been killed, they said. And not by a brute, not by a beast, not by a fish, they said, but by an intelligence.

He stove in Ahab's boat, and Ahab, brave man, dove after him, knife in hand, ready to die if he had to.

But he didn't have to. Moby-Dick took his leg and let him go. Let him go to live a life that would always be damaged, always crippled, always be a little smaller. Moby-Dick turned Ahab from a man to something less than a man.

Why white? So the whale is white, so what? Why is that important? I could tell you – I've certainly *thought* about it – but it's not important. For the men on the ship it was just something to add to the dread. Something's white, it seems mystical, seems beyond your grasp, seems unimaginable, ineffable.

So everyone was absolutely drunk on this idea. We were going to kill the white whale. It was dangerous, uneconomical, and made no sense, but we were going to do it. We were going to make the white whale spout black blood. And then that whale, that unknowable white whale, he would be ours. We would have him. It was worth nothing. But to us it was worth everything.

(The men can be heard again. Ad lib.)

1. You call that dancing? I'll dance on your grave!

2. Give over that pipe, Tash!

3. Pip Pip Pip! Dance and dance and dance again!

4. More grog! Where's the grog?

5. (to 6) C'mon! Join in!

6. Don't want to.

5. Why not?

6. I want to go home.

(General mood kill. 5 tries to pick it up.)

5. Home? Fuck home! Sail on, ship! Into the black night!

(It doesn't work. The mood is dead. Quiet.)

1. Weather's picking up.

2. Storm.

3. Storm.

5. Don't worry about a storm. Ahab kills storms! Sail the ship right into 'em, split 'em apart.

4. God! Feel that wind!

5. Don't stop dancing, Pip! Damn you!

2. The sky is so black.

4. See that? Lightning!

5. Shit.

(They listen. Thunder.)

6. Stations.

(They scatter.)

NINE

(Starbuck and Ahab in Ahab's cabin.)

STARBUCK. Sir, I must ask you –

AHAB. I have your answer already, Starbuck.

STARBUCK. But –

AHAB. "Sir, do you really think it's practical to spend an entire three-year whaling voyage searching for one whale? In all the oceans of the world, really sir, do you think that's prudent?" Am I close?

STARBUCK. Well –

AHAB. And here is your answer. (He produces a chart of the oceans.) This is *science*, Mr. Starbuck. Look. I've charted on this map every place that sperm whales have been reported killed according to the place and date of their deaths. Look at these patterns. This is science. I can predict where whales can be found, when they can be found there, how many can be found there, even in which direction they will be swimming.

This red line here is Moby-Dick. This is us right now. And right – here – is where we're going to kill him.

STARBUCK. There? But sir, we won't get there for eighteen months.

AHAB. I don't care if it takes eighteen *years*, Mr. Starbuck. We *will* find Moby-Dick. We will find him, we will catch him, we will kill him. Do you understand?

STARBUCK. But sir, to the exclusion of –

AHAB. Oh, Starbuck, Starbuck. We will still hunt whales, don't get me wrong. I have the men now, but I'm not so stupid as to think I could hang on to them 'til the South Pacific. Crazy but not stupid, eh Starbuck?

STARBUCK. Yes sir. I'll remember that.

TEN

(The deck.)

SAILOR. WHALES!!

(Alarum. Men prepare to lower the boats. A bustle of shouts
and activity.)

AHAB. Lower the boats! Kill the whales! (He bangs on a
hatch. A group of sinister-looking Chinese men clamber
out.) Fedallah! Let's go! Lower away!

(They exit, clambering to their boat. Stubb and Flask, at the
head of their own crews, watch incredulously.)

FLASK. Who the hell is that?

STUBB. I think you just answered your own question.

FLASK. Where did they come from?

STUBB. The Manillas, from the look of them.

FLASK. They're stowaways?

STUBB. Wouldn't go that far.

FLASK. Who *are* they?

STUBB. Ahab's crew, I'd say.

FLASK. He brought his own crew?

STUBB. Looks like it.

FLASK. Stowed in the hold?

STUBB. Looks like it.

FLASK. He had five Chinamen in the hold for six months?

STUBB. Stretches the old credulity, doesn't it?

FLASK. He can *do* that?

STUBB. He's the captain. He can do anything he wants.

FLASK. He can *do* that?

STUBB. He's done it.

FLASK. Bring his own men? He can *do* that?

STUBB. They're not men, Flask. Let's get lowered before the whales die of old age.

(Action sequence. They chase whales. The whales escape.)

ELEVEN

(Ishmael addresses the audience. In the background, Ahab confers with Fedallah.)

ISHMAEL. We sail on. Days, weeks, months. Calm and storm, fog and sun. The sailors gossip about Ahab's harpooner Fedallah. Some say he's the devil, keeps his tail curled up around his leg. Some say he's a million years old. Some say that he is the real captain of the ship, his mouth clamped to Ahab's ear. Ahab says he's using science to find the whales, but others say that it's just Fedallah, guiding his hand, pushing him toward the darkness.

One night, we see a spout. Big one. On the horizon. We think, this is it. Our hunt is over. We sail out to the spout, but then it's gone. Next night, the same thing. And the next. Every night. Midnight of course. And all over again. Ever on, into the night.

Many things happen. One day we come by a ship, the Albatross, that glides by as if we aren't there. One day we find a giant squid. One day we come by a ship called the Town-Ho.

They have a story about the white whale. You can bet Ahab is pleased about that.

And then one day we kill a whale. Stubb kills a whale. We hang its head from one side of the ship. As the killer, Stubb gets to have the first steak.

(Night. Stubb at the capstan, waiting for dinner. A sperm whale head hangs from one side of the ship.)

STUBB. Cook! Come on, bring me my steak out here, I'm freezin' to death! (Cook, an elderly black man, enters with a steak on a plate.) Well, please don't break your back or strain yourself in any way, cook, it's only my dinner that you're keeping me from, just get it the hell over here sometime before nineteen-hundred! Come on, I'm starving here, I'm going to keel over here, come *on*!

COOK. Sorry Mr. Stubb. Here you go.

STUBB. First cut off the whale is always the most tasty, eh cook? I guess you wouldn't know.

COOK. I don't catch 'em sir, I only cook 'em.

STUBB. Well let's see how you cooked *this* one – uh, no. No. Cook, this is no good. What did you – no. I'm sorry. This is no – I am so sorry you were born without a BRAIN, but if I've told you once, I mean come *on* –

COOK. Excuse me?

STUBB. Look at this! You ruined it! It's a piece of charcoal here!

COOK. I barely –

STUBB. You barely *thought* is what you – Look. Here is the way you cook a whale-steak. You take the piece of meat –

this, by the way, is the piece of meat – and you *show* it the fire. Then you put it on a plate. Do you *got* that? Is that so *hard*? Can you even *conceive* of – what the hell is that *noise*?

COOK. The sharks, sir, at the carcass –

STUBB. You blithering idiot, I know what it *is*, why do they have to be so God-damned *loud*? I'm trying to eat here like a decent civilized human being and I can't even hear myself *chew* –

COOK. Sorry –

STUBB. Well go and talk to 'em, would ya?

COOK. What?

STUBB. Are you going deaf now too? Go *talk* to them, tell 'em to shut the hell up for a few minutes, Christ!

COOK. T-talk to the sharks?

STUBB. You *are* going deaf. Yes! God damn it, tell the fucking sharks to shut *up*! Move!

(Pause.)

COOK. All right… (He goes to the rail, addresses the sharks.) Hey! Sharks! Knock it off with the racket! Mr. Stubb's trying to eat!

STUBB. They can eat all they want, but they have to keep it down.

COOK. You can eat all you want, but stop smackin' your lips so damn loud!

STUBB. Cook! Hey!

COOK. Yes?

STUBB. You can't *swear* at them.

COOK. Excuse me?

STUBB. "Excuse me", listen to this guy – You can't convert sinners by *swearing* at them.

(Pause.)

COOK. I'm going.

STUBB. No, keep talking to them. *Coax* them.

(Pause. Cook tries again.)

COOK. Look. Sharks. Um, beloved sharks. Um, I know that, um, you are by nature, um, voracious. But you've got to – hey! Stop the damn tail-slapping when I'm talking to you! You can't hear me if you're slappin' your damn tail!

STUBB. Not with the swearing! Come *on*. Con*vince* them.

(Pause. Cook tries again.)

COOK. Ahem. My, my dear voracious creatures. Um, I, I don't *blame* you for your, your nature, but, but you've got to learn to *control* your, your nature. If you can, can control the, the shark inside you, you will be like, like *angels*. An angel is only a shark under control. Don't tear that blubber out of your neighbor's mouth. That's *wrong*. This whale, this whale doesn't even *belong* to you! Some of you bigger sharks, tear off some meat for the smaller boys!

STUBB. Now that's Christianity! Keep going!

COOK. B-but they're not listening.

STUBB. No?

COOK. They don't have ears to hear, Mr. Stubb. They only

have bellies. And when their bellies are full, they go to sleep on the coral and then they never hear anything.

STUBB. True. True. Then give the benediction and let me eat.

COOK. Cursed creatures! Make all the noise of hell! Eat your fill, burst your bellies and die!

STUBB. Amen.

COOK. (to Stubb) You're more shark than them.

STUBB. And good night.

(Blackout.)

TWELVE

(Ishmael addresses the audience.)

ISMAEL. A while later, we come across another ship. The Jeroboam. This boat has a crazy man on board. The crazy man is under the impression that he is the archangel Gabriel. The funny part is that everyone else on the ship believes him. Seems a plague broke out on the ship and everyone who believed him didn't die. So now this Gabriel fella is kind of running things on that ship.

They sent a boat out to us, and Ahab went to meet them.

(Two whaling boats on the ocean. Captain Mayhew, oarsman, Gabriel in one, Ahab and oarsman in the other. The sound of waves is loud; they have to shout to hear each other.)

MAYHEW. Don't come any closer! Infection!

AHAB. I'm not scared of your epidemic, come aboard!

GABRIEL. Think of the fevers! Yellow and bilious! Beware of the plague!

MAYHEW. I'll handle this, Gabriel –

AHAB. Have you seen the white whale?

GABRIEL. Think of your whale-boat! Stoven and sunk! Beware the tail!

MAYHEW. Gabriel, please –

AHAB. Have you seen the white whale!

MAYHEW. I have seen the white whale!

GABRIEL. Turn back! I warned him and he didn't listen! Now I'm warning you!

AHAB. Tell that miserable cretin to shut up and finish your story!

MAYHEW. Two years out we saw him!

GABRIEL. I told him not to go after the white whale!

MAYHEW. I got five men to go out with me! I finally got an iron in him!

AHAB. Then what?

GABRIEL. He's the incarnation of the Shaker God!

AHAB. Shut up, you moron! -- Then what?

MAYHEW. My mate, Macey, had him in his sights! He was just about to hurl when the whale knocked him clear out of the boat! We never saw him again! Are you hunting the white whale?

AHAB. Until I die!

GABRIEL. Think of the blasphemer! Drowned and dead! Beware the wrath of God!

MAYHEW. We have to get back to the ship!

AHAB. Wait! Before you go, we got a letter when we left Nantucket! It's addressed to someone on your ship!

MAYHEW. Who is it for?

AHAB. It's – oarsman, give me that letter – it says "Mr. Harry...Mr. Harry, yes, Macey, Ship Jeroboam..." What?

MAYHEW. Macey! That was my mate! That's the man who went over!

AHAB. It's from his wife! Do you want it?

GABRIEL. You keep it! You'll be seeing him sooner than us! (to oarsman) Back to the ship!

(They pull away.)

AHAB. Damn you! Damn you Gabriel! I'll see you in Hell!

(Blackout.)

THIRTEEN

(Stubb, Flask, others, hoist a right whale head up the other side of the ship. Fedallah and Ahab confer to one side.)

STUBB. What does Ahab want with this thing? We're a sperm whale fishery, we don't have time to go after these useless things!

FLASK. Don't you know? They say that a ship that hoists the head of a spermaceti on its starboard side and the head of a right whale on the port, that ship will never capsize.

STUBB. No. I've never heard that. In all my years I never heard that particular nugget of maritime folklore. Where did *you* hear it?

FLASK. I heard it from Fedallah. He told Ahab.

STUBB. Fedallah? This is *his* idea?

FLASK. He seems to know a lot about whales…

STUBB. Of course he does, he's evil incarnate, why not?

FLASK. Oh, he gives me the creeps, that's for sure. You ever notice that tusk of his is carved into, looks like a snake head?

STUBB. Hell, I don't even look at him. His tail down his pants like it is, you know he sleeps in his boots so we can't see the hoofs.

FLASK. What's the old man see in him?

STUBB. I suppose one could say they have a bargain.

FLASK. What kind of – oh. Never mind. How old do you think he is, Fedallah?

STUBB. Old as time, Flask. That's the whole point. I say we throw him overboard.

FLASK. But if he's the devil, what good is –

STUBB. Give him a good dunking anyway.

FLASK. Yeah, but he'd come back and dunk you for good.

STUBB. He tries it, I'll knock his tooth out.

(Unseen by Stubb, Fedallah comes to stand right next to the pair.)

Give him a pair of black eyes. You think I'm afraid of him? I'll wrap his tail around the capstan so tight it'll snap off – Oh hi, Fedallah.

(Blackout.)

FOURTEEEN

(Ishmael addresses the audience.)

ISHMAEL.

Now I could tell you about whales. I know about whales. I've read all about whales. I've seen them, I've touched them, I've swam with them, I've dissected them, I've hacked them into pieces and melted down their blubber. I could tell you about whales. I could talk your ear off about whales. I could go on for a good long time about whales: how to catch them, how to kill them, how to turn them into oil, what they eat, how they swim, peculiarities of their behavior, everything.

But in the end, the fact remains: I know nothing about whales. No one knows anything about whales. Whales are, unfortunately, unknowable. That fish we haul up the side of the ship, that's not a whale, that's just a husk, just a shell. Even that fish that we chase through the foaming seas, risking our necks ten times a second, that's not a whale, that's not what a whale is, that's only the time that we *see* them.

So no. I can't tell you about the whale, about leviathan. It can't be told. I don't know how they act, what they think or feel, or even, truly, what they look like, since I never see them where they live. Leviathan is the one creature that must remain unpainted to the last.

SAILOR. (oov) WHALES!! WHALES!!

(Lights up. Stubb and crew in a whale boat, including Pip and Dagoo. They have an iron in the whale and are being towed by it.)

STUBB. Row! Row, you sons-of-bachelors! For God's sake please don't *hurt* yourselves, ladies! Please don't get any blisters on your poor delicate fingers or you won't be able to work the crochet hooks! Just break your fucking backs and kill that fucking whale! Who the hell are you?

OARSMAN. That's Pip, Mr. Stubb.

STUBB. What the hell is this boy doing steering my fucking whale-boat?

OARSMAN. Regular man is sick, Mr. Stubb.

STUBB. So they give me a *boy*?

OARSMAN. He'll be fine, Mr. Stubb.

PIP. I can do it, Mr. Stubb.

STUBB. You'd *better*, I don't have time to bother! *Row*, you lazy bastards! The whale is over *there*, morons! Faster! Faster! Oh please don't break a *sweat* or anything just because your *life* depends on it –

(The boat pitches. Pip falls overboard.)

DAGOO. Cut! Cut!

STUBB. Cut what? What the fuck!

DAGOO. Man overboard!

STUBB. Where? Who?

OARSMAN. Pip, Mr. Stubb!

STUBB. I thought you said *man*, Dagoo! Keep rowing, you bastards!

OARSMAN. We should stop for him, Mr. Stubb! He won't last long out here!

STUBB. You're joking. Right? You're joking with me. You're having a little joke at my expense. You're dallying with my sense of propriety for the sake of humor.

OARSMAN. We really should, Mr. –

STUBB. Oh, Fuck it then! Cut! Cut the line! Let's stop to pick up the black child!

(They cut the line and pull Pip out of the water.)

DAGOO. Here you go, Pip. That will do it.

PIP. Thank you sir. Thank you Mr. Stubb.

STUBB. Let's get one thing straight here, son. This time I was intoxicated by the milk of human kindness. Next time you die. Just one barrel of oil from that whale is worth more than what I'd get for you on an auction block in Alabama. Do you understand?

PIP. Yes Mr. Stubb. I'm sorry Mr. Stubb.

STUBB. Now sit down and hang on. (to others) ROW, YOU COCKSUCKERS! We ain't got all day!

(They row. Pip, who has not had time to sit down, immediately falls overboard.)

DAGOO. Man overboard!

STUBB. What?!

DAGOO. Pip, Mr. Stubb!

STUBB. What the – keep going!

DAGOO. Mr. Stubb –

STUBB. Keep rowing, you motherfuckers! I told him the deal, Dagoo! It's his own fucking fault! Now if *you* want to jump out and save him, do it now and lighten my fucking load! If not, sit the fuck down and shut the fuck up!

(Dagoo starts, then thinks better of it. The boat is rowed off. Pip bobs up and down in the water.)

PIP. Hello? Mr. Stubb? I'm sorry. Pip's sorry. Hello? Mr. Stubb? Mr. Stubb? Anybody? Hello?

(Blackout.)

FIFTEEN

(The deck. Starbuck addresses Ishmael and some other men. There is a vat of spermaceti.)

STARBUCK. Men, this is sperm. This is what we're here for. This substance is secreted by a special gland unique to the spermaceti whale. Hence the name. It is the most valuable substance found in the ocean. When we get back to Nantucket, it will make us all a lot of money.

But before that happens, someone has to squeeze out the lumps. That is your job today. No machine has yet been built which can do this job as efficiently a man's hands. So hunker down by this vat and squeeze yourself some sperm.

(They do. Starbuck exits.)

ISHMAEL. Well. This is peculiar. I don't think I've ever felt anything like this before. Hm. It, it's quite nice, isn't it?

SAILOR. Mm.

ISHMAEL. It's so, so slick. So sweet. My fingers feel like eels. I can see why this stuff is so popular.

SAILOR. Hm.

ISHMAEL. Huh. This is – huh. You know, I'm sitting here, squeezing sperm, on this beautiful deck under this beautiful sun on this beautiful day, and, and I can't think of anything I'd rather be doing. You know? And I don't mean that figuratively. I mean I literally can't think of anything. I mean, like, ever. You know? Smells like violets. Don't you think? Violets?

SAILOR. Hm.

ISHMAEL. It just – it feels, it feels…great. Doesn't it. I could definitely do this all day long. Squeeze, squeeze, squeeze. Wow. This is great. I, I think I'm getting kind of a buzz going here. This feels so great.

SAILOR. That's my hand.

ISHMAEL. Oh. Sorry.

SAILOR. It's all right.

ISHMAEL. I –

SAILOR. It's really all right.

ISHMAEL. I didn't mean –

SAILOR. I really don't mind if you keep doing it.

ISHMAEL. I – right. I'm trying to think of something that's given me more pleasure than this. And I can't. I can't think of anything.

SAILOR. Me neither.

ISHMAEL. You know what? This is heaven. This is heaven. When I get to heaven, what I'm going to see is long rows of angels, each with their hands in a jar of sperm.

(Blackout.)

SIXTEEN

(Ahab's cabin.)

AHAB. Who is it? Get the hell out of here.

STARBUCK. It's me, captain.

AHAB. What is it, Starbuck?

STARBUCK. The oil in the hold is leaking. We're going to have to stop in Japan and fix it.

AHAB. Are you crazy? Stop now? Are you crazy? Go away.

STARBUCK. We have to stop, sir. Or we'll lose more oil in one day that we could make up in a year.

AHAB. What do I care? Let it leak.

STARBUCK. Captain, we've come twenty thousand miles for that oil.

AHAB. We've come twenty thousand miles for only one thing, Mr. Starbuck, and I'm not going to stop for anything now. The hold has a leak? I have a leak, Mr. Starbuck. I'm *full* of leaks. I have a leak in my heart, I have a leak in my head. I'm draining away, into the mouth of that whale. I've already lost my leg. Either I stop *that* leak or I drain away completely.

STARBUCK. Sir, the owners –

AHAB. Fuck the owners. Starbuck. Fuck the owners. What are they going to do? "Complain"? They can stand on the beach of Nantucket and scream their faces blue, I'll never hear them. Owners? Owners? Who owns this ship, Starbuck? Who owns this ship? I do. I own this ship and you know it. On deck, Mr. Starbuck.

STARBUCK. Sir. In the past you have been a good captain. A great captain.

AHAB. On deck, Mr. Starbuck.

STARBUCK. And perhaps you will one day again –

(Ahab grabs his musket and points it at Starbuck.)

AHAB. Get one thing clear, Mr. Starbuck. One God rules this earth, and one man rules the Pequod. On deck.

STARBUCK. You have outraged me, captain, not insulted me. I will no longer disagree with you or stand in your way. You have no reason to fear Starbuck. But perhaps you have reason to fear yourself.

AHAB. Ahab fear Ahab? (Pause.) You know, you might have something there, old tar. (He puts down the gun.) Fine. Up Burtons, find the leak.

STARBUCK. Thank you sir.

AHAB. You're a good man, Starbuck.

STARBUCK. Thank you sir.

SEVENTEEN

(Queequeg's cabin. Queequeg lies ill in his hammock. Ishmael, Pip, Starbuck, others.)

QUEEQUEG. I'm dying, friend.

ISHMAEL. You're not dying.

QUEEQUEG. I'm dying. I know when I'm dying.

ISHMAEL. You're not dying.

QUEEQUEG. It was cleaning out the hold. Looking for the leak. That's what it was. That's what killed me.

ISHMAEL. Queequeg –

QUEEQUEG. This fever. Finally did me in. Finally did in Queequeg. Is my coffin done?

ISHMAEL. You don't need a coffin.

QUEEQUEG. Is it done?

ISHMAEL. It's done. It's finished.

QUEEQUEG. Put me in it. I'm ready to die.

(His coffin is brought in. Queequeg is placed in it.)

PIP. Poor Queequeg. Poor wanderer. Never resting. Now you'll wander on forever.

If you get to the Antilles, where the sun always shines on a fine lazy beach, keep an eye out for a sad little black boy named Pip. He went out looking for whales and didn't come back. I think maybe he washed up there in the Antilles. If you find him, comfort him. He must be very sad; look, he forgot his tambourine.

You go and die, Queequeg. I'll beat out your death march on the black boy's forgotten tambourine.

ISHMAEL. (to Queequeg) How is it?

QUEEQUEG. It will do.

STARBUCK. Pip? Are you all right?

ISHMAEL. He hasn't been himself since the day he fell out of Stubb's boat.

STARBUCK. I can see that he's not himself. I'm wondering who the hell he *is*.

PIP. Give Queequeg his harpoon. Lay it across his chest. Queequeg dies a brave man! Better than Pip, who died a whining, mewling coward. Queequeg, if you find Pip in the Antilles, give him a kick for me. Tell everybody in the Antilles that Pip's a coward. Jumped from a whale-boat! Shame on cowards! Let 'em drown! Shame! Shame!

QUEEQUEG. You know what?

ISHMAEL. What? What is it, Queequeg?

QUEEQUEG. I…I actually feel better.

ISHMAEL. What?

STARBUCK. It's the fever. He's hallucinating. I've seen it a hundred times. He's not got long now.

QUEEQUEG. Um…no. No. I actually feel quite a bit better.

ISHMAEL. Is that possible?

STARBUCK. Impossible.

QUEEQUEG. Yes. I feel…I feel fine now. Yes. I actually feel fine now. Yes. In fact, if it's all right with you, I think I'll go back to work. Is that all right?

(Blackout.)

EIGHTEEN

(The forge. Carpenter hammers a pike. Ahab looks on.)

AHAB. Those sparks. So beautiful. And so hot. But look at you. Not a mark on you.

CARPENTER. On me it's *all* scars, captain. You can't scar a scar.

AHAB. You sound very sane to me, carpenter. I don't like it. Madness likes company. What are you making?

CARPENTER. I'm welding a pike-head. There were some seams and dents in it.

AHAB. And you'll make it all smooth again?

CARPENTER. That's the job.

AHAB. I'll bet you could smooth out seams in anything, couldn't you?

CARPENTER. I think I can, sir. Every seam but one.

AHAB. Could you smooth out this seam in my forehead? If

you could do that? If you could do that, I would put my head on your anvil right now and you could hit it with your heaviest hammer.

CARPENTER. Sorry sir – that's the one.

AHAB. Yes. That is the one. Isn't it. You're right; it cannot be smoothed. This wrinkle is no longer just on my skin; it's in my bone. It's in my brain. My *brain* is wrinkled. My *brain* is dented.

But enough. No more gaffs and pikes today. I need you to make me a harpoon. The strongest ever made. One that will stick in a whale like his own fin-bone. (He produces a leather bag.) This is a bag of nails. Steel nails from the shoes of race-horses.

CARPENTER. That's the toughest material on earth.

AHAB. And they will weld together like glue from a murderer's bones. Can you do it?

(ISHMAEL appears, addresses the audience.)

ISHMAEL. And so it is done.

(Ahab holds the finished harpoon.)

AHAB. Splendid! Now the shaft. Hammer out twelve rods. Wind the twelve rods together like a rope, and hammer them into one. Quick! I'll blow the fire.

ISHMAEL. And so it is done.

(Ahab holds the finished staff.)

AHAB. Perfect!

CARPENTER. Captain, sir. Is this the iron for the white whale?

AHAB. Yes! God's blood, yes! Now for the barbs. These are my razors. Take them. Don't look at me like that, I'm never going to need them again. I'm not going to eat, shave or pray until Moby-Dick is dead.

ISHMAEL. And so it is done.

(Carpenter finishes attaching the barbs.)

CARPENTER. It's done. Bring the water over here.

AHAB. No. Water's no good. Blood. It has to be blood. Get me the harpooneers!

ISHMAEL. And the harpooneers come, and cut open their arms, and fill a cup full of blood. And they use the blood to temper the barbs.

(Queequeg, Tashtego, Dagoo and Fedallah all stand around Ahab, who hold a cup of their blood.)

AHAB. I baptize you in the name of the father and in the name of the devil!

(He puts the harpoon in the blood. It hisses. Blackout.)

NINETEEN

(A ship, the Rachel, pulls up alongside the Pequod.)

SAILOR. A ship! A ship!

(Activity. The crew comes out on deck. Ahab stands at the rail. The captain of the Rachel, Gardiner, and his mates appear at their rail.)

STARBUCK. It's the Rachel. Out of Nantucket.

AHAB. That would be Gardiner. (to Gardiner) Have you seen the white whale?

GARDINER. Ahab! Thank God!

AHAB. Have you seen the white whale?

GARDINER. Yesterday – have you seen a whale boat?

AHAB. Yesterday! Where? Where was he? Not killed! You didn't kill him, did you? What happened?

GARDINER. Have you seen a whale boat? We lost a whale boat. Will you help us search?

AHAB. Where exactly did you see the whale?

GARDINER. We have to find that whale boat! Please help us find it! It's very important!

STUBB. What was on it? Your watch?

(Everyone on the Pequod laughs.)

GARDINER. My son.

(The laughter dies.)

My boy. My boy was in that boat. Please. Please help me find him. It's been almost a day and we can't find him. Please help us look for him. Me. Help me. I beg you. We have to –

AHAB. WHERE EXACTLY DID YOU SEE THE WHITE WHALE?

GARDINER. I'll, I'll charter your ship! I'll pay for it, I don't care what it costs. You have to help me. You have to.

SAILOR. His son is dead. They're all dead.

AHAB. (to Starbuck) What do you suppose is this man's problem that he can't answer a simple question?

GARDINER. Just say yes. Just tell me yes. You must say yes to me. I won't go until you say yes. The golden rule. Sir. Captain Ahab. Your own boy. Your own child. Safe at home. What do you say? What is your answer?

STARBUCK. (to Ahab) Shall I give orders to follow her, sir?

AHAB. Why isn't he telling me what I want to know?

GARDINER. What is your answer?

AHAB. My answer is no. Captain Gardiner, I'm losing time.

Good bye. Good bye and God bless you. I have to go. Mr.
Starbuck! The binnacle!

(He exits. Everyone watches him go. There's a sick pause.
Gardiner steps down from his rail, almost falling. His mates
help him away. The Rachel glides away slowly as everyone
watches. Fade out.)

TWENTY

(The deck. Typhoon. Action. Men scurry about. Rigging. Alarum.)

STUBB. (singing) Oh! Jolly is the gale, and a joker is the whale, a'flourishing his tail – such a funny, sporty, gamy, jesty, jokey, hokey-pokey lad is the ocean, oh!

STARBUCK. Can it with the singing, Stubb! The typhoon is singing hard enough!

STUBB. I'll stop singing when you cut my throat, Mr. Starbuck! And I'll sing you the doxology for the wind-up!

STARBUCK. You're as crazy as Ahab!

STUBB. Where the hell is all this wind coming from?

STARBUCK. It's from the east! Look! If we can turn the ship around, it'll blow us all the way back home!

STUBB. How the hell can you tell which direction it is?!

STARBUCK. The quadrant! (He produces a quadrant.) I'm going to chart us a course to turn us around and get us the hell out of here! We're heading right into the storm! We have to –

(Ahab appears, carrying his harpoon.)

AHAB. Yes! The quadrant! I've been looking for that! (He takes it from Starbuck.) The quadrant! The direction-finder! The useless toy! Don't you agree that the quadrant is useless, Mr. Starbuck?! What can it tell you? Nothing!

STARBUCK. It tells you where you are!

AHAB. What kind of idiot needs to know that?! I know EXACTLY where I am! I'm RIGHT HERE! I'm RIGHT HERE! This toy can't tell me what I NEED! It can't tell me where one grain of sand, one puff of cloud will be TOMOR-ROW, and it can't tell me where to find the white whale! It's useless! It's a useless toy!

(He smashes it on the deck. He addresses the sky.)

OLD THUNDER! IT'S ME! IT'S AHAB! HERE IS MY ROD! THE HARPOON THAT WILL KILL MOBY-DICK!

(Thunder. Lightning. The masts glow with St. Elmo's fire.)

STARBUCK. The masts! Captain, look!

STUBB. St. Elmo's fire!

(The sailors fall silent before the spectacle.)

STARBUCK. God have mercy on us all!

AHAB. YES! LOOK AT THE FLAME! THE WHITE FLAME THAT POINTS THE WAY TO THE WHITE WHALE! (to sky) HEAVENLY FIRE! (to a sailor) Hand me that chain! I want to *feel* this. Blood against fire!

(He is handed a chain which is attached to the mast and also glows.)

HEAVENLY FIRE! I WORSHIPPED YOU UNTIL YOU STRUCK ME AND SCARRED MY ENTIRE BODY FOR EVER! NOW I KNOW THAT WORSHIP IS NOT WHAT YOU WANT FROM ME, BUT DEFIANCE! YOU PUNISH THOSE WHO LOVE YOU, STRIKE THOSE WHO WORSHIP YOU, AND KILL THOSE WHO HATE YOU! I OWN YOUR SPEECHLESS, PLACELESS POWER NOW, BUT I WILL, UNTIL THE LAST GASP OF MY EARTHQUAKE LIFE, DEFY YOUR MASTERY OVER ME! YOUR POWER GAVE ME LIFE! YOU BREATHED YOUR FIRE INTO ME, AND NOW I BREATHE IT BACK AT YOU!!

(Lightning strikes the mast, several times. Ahab does not move.)

DON'T YOU SEE? *I OWN YOUR POWER!!* BLIND ME AND I WILL STILL GROPE, BURN ME AND I WILL STILL BE ASHES!! YOU ARE LIGHT LEAPING OUT OF DARKNESS, BUT I AM DARKNESS LEAPING OUT OF LIGHT! LEAP! LEAP UP AND LICK THE SKY! LET ME BE WELDED TO YOU! DEFYINGLY I WORSHIP YOU!!

(Lightning strikes and fire shoots out the end of the harpoon.)

STARBUCK. God's against you, old man! Stop this voyage now! Let's turn back and go home!

(Ahab throws the chain down. The harpoon remains on fire.)

AHAB. (to the crew) All of your oaths to kill the white whale are as binding as mine! If you still have fears, I will now blow them out!

(He blows on the harpoon, which immediately extinguishes. Blackout.)

TWENTY-ONE

(Night. Ahab's cabin. Ahab is asleep. Starbuck stands next to him, holding his musket.)

STARBUCK. He was going to shoot me. With this gun. Look at me. I've handled guns a hundred times, and now I'm shaking like a leaf. Is it loaded? Yes. It's loaded. Should I unload it? Perhaps. Perhaps.

This gun. He was going to kill me with this gun. This one right here. The one I'm holding. Right here. He would have killed me. He *will* kill me. He'll kill me. He'll kill the whole crew. He'll kill the whole crew. He smashed the quadrant, the typhoon ruined the compass, we're groping around blind. He will murder all of us. Thirty-odd men. Should I stop him?

He's talking in his sleep. But at least he's asleep. Which is the only way I can deal with him.

What could we do with him? What are my options? We could, what, tie him up? Put him in a cage? I'd like to see somebody try. Hell, even if we succeeded, we'd all be driven mad by his ravings before we ever saw land again.

I put the muzzle against his head. One touch, and I get to hug my wife and child again. God help me. Please help me.

(Ahab speaks in his sleep.)

AHAB. Moby-Dick! I clutch your heart at last!

(Starbuck jumps, wrestles with the gun. It looks like he's wrestling with an angel. He puts it back in its rack.)

STARBUCK. God help us all.

TWENTY-TWO

(On deck. It's a beautiful day.)

AHAB. Starbuck!

STARBUCK. Sir.

AHAB. Isn't it a beautiful day?

STARBUCK. Yes it is sir.

AHAB. Look at that sky.

STARBUCK. It's beautiful sir.

AHAB. It was a day just like this – just like this – I was eighteen – eighteen! Imagine being eighteen! Forty years. Forty years since I killed my first whale.

Forty years I've been on this water. Not three on land. Forty years I've eaten salted fish and hardtack while the poorest farmer on land had fresh fruit and warm bread. Married. Married one night, somewhere in there. One night before setting out. One night. One dent in my marriage pillow. Wife – wife! She's a widow. She's a widow. Forty years I've been chasing this fish and my wife's a widow. Forty years. A thousand lowerings. When would it be enough, do you suppose? To say enough. To say I'm finished.

What a fool I am. What a fool. Forty years and what? Am I a richer man? A better man? Christ, what a burden. And me with only one leg to carry it. Do I look so old? Starbuck? I feel as old as Adam. All of history piled up on my shoulders.

Brush my hair out of my eyes, would you? I think it's making me cry.

Let me look at you. Let me look you in the eye. It's better to look into a human eye than to stare at the sea. Or the sky. Or God.

I see land in your eye. The green land. My wife and child. I see my wife and child in your eye.

Starbuck, do something for me. When we find the whale, you don't go. You don't go. You stay. You stay on the Pequod. This is my fight. This is mine. I will go to Moby-Dick. You will go back to the home I see in your eye.

STARBUCK. Captain, why does *anyone* have to chase that horrible fish? Anyone. You *have* done enough. This is already enough. A hundred times, a thousand times over, you've done enough. Don't you think? And on this day, on this beautiful day, this perfect day, let's just thank God for what we still have and just go home. We can do that. Let's just go. We can just turn around and do it. You tell me and I tell the men and we just do it. Just forget about the damn fish. Let it go on, doing what it does, it's not our business. Let it keep going on, scaring sailors and making us wonder just what the hell it was all about. We can do that, can't we? We can live with that, can't we? We can do it right now. This can all end. All this. All this hate, all this madness, all this horrible waste.

It can all end. Right now. This instant. And back to
Nantucket. Good old Nantucket, good old stupid backwards
Nantucket. You tell me, and I tell the men, and we're on our
way home. Can you imagine that? Happily, hysterically, on
our way home. Home. Your family, my family, old age.
Loving, longing, paternal old age. And telling your grand-
children your unbelievable tales of the sea. Sir. Captain. My
captain. Surely, every now and then, they must have days like
this in Nantucket.

AHAB. They do. They do. Summers. In the morning. My
boy wakes up from his noontime nap and his mother tells
him about his crazy old cannibal father. He's at sea now, but
one day he'll come back to dance him again.

STARBUCK. My Mary! That's my Mary exactly! Every day,
she promised, she takes my boy to the hill, to be the first to
see my sail.

AHAB. Yes.

STARBUCK. Then that's it. We head for Nantucket. I'll
chart out a course right now and we'll do it. Can you see
your boy's face in the window? My boy's hand on the hill?

AHAB. Yes. Yes.

STARBUCK. Give me the order. We'll be home tomorrow,
your face in your young wife's hair.

AHAB. I know what you're saying. Starbuck. I do. Why am I
doing this? I don't have an answer. I don't know. I'll gladly
tell you I don't know. This isn't me. I'm not the one doing
this. I would never do this. I have no answers; I only have
questions.

Is Ahab Ahab? Who moves this arm? Me? God? Or who?
Does the sun move itself? Do the stars revolve in the sky on

their own, or does God move them? And if God moves the heavens, then what am I? How can this one small heart beat, this one small brain think, unless God does that beating, does that thinking, does that living?

Smell that wind. It smells like a meadow. Somewhere they're making hay in the shadows of the Alps, sleeping in the new-mown grass under the noon-day sun. But one day we all sleep. No matter how hard we work, one day we all lie down and sleep in the field.

(He sees something, off.)

What is that? Did you see that? Call all hands! Did you see that? Look! It's his hump! It's his white hump! All hands! THE WHALE!

(Blackout.)

TWENTY-THREE

(Ishmael addresses the audience.)

ISHMAEL. This story is over. Ahab saw the whale first, and so the gold coin was his.

Three days we chased the whale. And I have to say, it was something. How it moved through the water. Impossible to describe. Glided. A mild joyousness. Very quick, but very still. A great form, cutting through the waves with an unknowable somnolence. It was hypnotic. We couldn't stop. None of us. No one complained after that. After seeing it. No one blamed Ahab any more, no one thought he was crazy any more. Not after seeing the thing. We all worked as one in pursuit of the whale. We couldn't stop. We knew what waited for us, and we couldn't stop.

(In dumbshow, boats chase Moby-Dick through the water.)

We lowered the boats and chased the whale through the water. After a time, the whale turned and attacked.

(Moby-Dick comes up from the water, knocking the boat out of the water, throwing men in every direction.)

He wrecked the boat, but no one was hurt. We got back on the Pequod and chased it for another day. On the next lowering, he smashed the boat, broke off Ahab's ivory leg, and took Fedallah down with him.

(We see this as well.)

Again, Starbuck begged Ahab to stop. And once again, Ahab insisted that it wasn't his decision to make.

And on the third day, Ahab took a boat into the water again. I was in the boat with him. We chased the whale, Ahab, his crew and me. We got a ways out, and then the whale turned and swam back towards the ship. Next thing we knew, the Pequod was sinking. Moby-Dick had stove in its side. And the Pequod sank without a trace. Almost without a trace.

That got Ahab mad. He threw his lance at the whale, and it stuck. By God it stuck. And it stuck hard. The whale pulled us, surging through the waves, so hard, so fast that I fell out of the boat, just like poor little Pip. I bobbed up and down in the water and watched as the whale pulled Ahab's boat, Ahab, who looked victorious at last. But as Ahab's line went out, it got caught around his neck, snapped it in two, pulled him over. And that was that. The last of Ahab.

(We have watched the above happen in silence. Now our focus returns to Ishmael.)

And everyone died. As you know. Except me. The only thing left of the Pequod was Queequeg's coffin. After he decided not to die, we had sealed it, caulked it, and used it for a lifebuoy. Indeed.

And so I drifted. A day and a night. The sharks swam by with padlocks on their mouths. Then the Rachel, still looking for her lost children, found another orphan.

(Blackout. End of play.)

Made in United States
North Haven, CT
31 January 2023